HOW TO BE AN AWESOME TODDLER

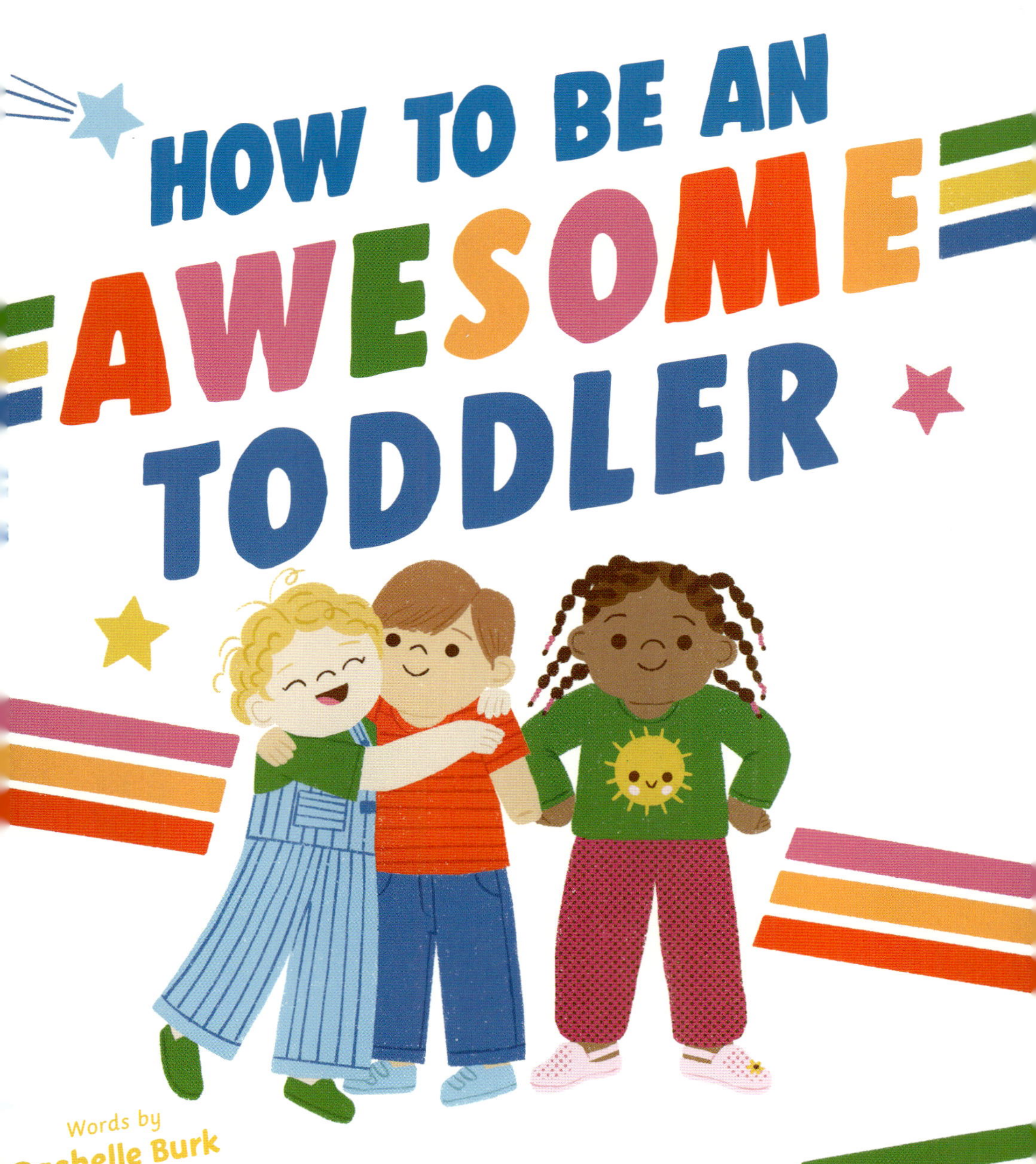

Words by
Rachelle Burk

Pictures by
Denise Holmes

50 Easy Rhymes to Make Growing Up Exciting and Fun!

HOW TO BE AN AWESOME TODDLER

50 Easy Rhymes to Make Growing Up Exciting and Fun!

Words by
Rachelle Burk

Pictures by
Denise Holmes

sourcebooks eXplore

CONTENTS

SAFETY

SOCIAL SKILLS: ACTIONS

INTRODUCTION

A LETTER TO CAREGIVERS

The fleeting and precious toddler stage is when your little ones are blossoming into their unique selves. It's a time of boundless exploration, where every experience is a learning opportunity for both you and your child. The days may seem endless, exhilarating, and exhausting, but these moments will pass in the blink of an eye. You can make the most of this time by establishing nurturing rhythms, routines, and relationships. With gentle guidance and loving boundaries, you can help your child grow strong, healthy, and kind.

More than anything, remember *you've got this*! You are your child's safe haven, their guide, and their biggest cheerleader. Embrace the chaos, find joy in the little moments, and know that this developmental phase is laying the foundation for the amazing person your toddler will become!

FOR ALL TODDLERS

Every child needs to learn essential skills and habits to take with them throughout their lives. This book is designed to provide age-appropriate lessons on health and hygiene, social skills, and safety.

Each page of this book is thoughtfully crafted with three engaging elements:

THE RHYME: Catchy poems make it easy for little ones to memorize and internalize the lessons.

THE TAKEAWAYS: Engaging explanations and examples provide further context and understanding.

THE CONVERSATION: Questions for the child encourage connection, conversation, and application of the concepts.

EXPLORING ESSENTIAL LIFE SKILLS

Throughout this book, you and your child will explore a wide range of topics crucial for their development and well-being:

HEALTH AND HYGIENE:
From handwashing to dental care, these habits promote physical health and prevent the spread of illness.

SOCIAL SKILLS:
Learning to share, take turns, and express emotions in healthy ways fosters positive relationships and emotional intelligence.

SAFETY:
Awareness of potential dangers and appropriate responses can help keep your child safe.

ANYTIME READING

Read this book to your child any time, not just when addressing a specific behavior or issue. Toddlers will delight in the rhymes and illustrations, making it a perfect addition to your regular story-time routine. Invite your child to learn about habits and skills in a relaxed, enjoyable setting, separate from moments of correction or discipline.

FLEXIBLE AND ENGAGING

There's no "right way" to read this book. You can read it straight through or hop around, focusing on the skills your child needs to cultivate or the poems they love best. The interactive nature of the book encourages active participation and engagement from both you and your little one.

We hope this book becomes a cherished companion on your caretaking journey, helping you instill essential life skills in your toddler while creating lasting memories and strengthening your bond. Happy reading!

BRUSHING TEETH

Twice a day I brush my teeth—
up, down, left and right.
I rinse and spit, and then I show
my smile, sparkly white!

Brushing every morning and before bed will keep my teeth and gums healthy. I even brush my tongue!

If you could choose any flavor for your toothpaste, what would it be?

BRUSHING HAIR

When tufts of hair are sticking out,

way up in the air,

I comb out all the tangles...

and now I love my hair!

Tangled hair can hurt! It feels good when I fix my hair every day, and I look better too.

What are your favorite ways to wear your hair?

GETTING DRESSED

When I wake I put on clothes.
That's how I start the day.
Socks and undies, shirt and pants...
I'm ready now to play!

It's fun to be part of picking out my clothes each day. I can get dressed by myself, but sometimes I ask for help.

What is your favorite outfit and why?

EATING HEALTHY FOODS

How can I grow big and strong?

Eat vegetables and cheese.

Have rice and beans with fish and meat.

Chomp fruits and nuts and seeds!

What are your favorite healthy foods?

TRYING NEW FOODS

Slice it. Peel it. Spread or mash it.

Toast or bake or fry it.

Perhaps I won't like every food,

but once, at least, I'll try it.

Even if some foods look yucky, they might taste delicious. I'll never know unless I try.

What foods do your friends like that you don't? What foods do you like that your friends don't?

USING THE POTTY

This is what I need to do
when I have to "go":
I hurry to the potty
and there, I let it flow!

I feel like a big kid when I go to the potty on my own. I wipe myself and wash my hands when I'm finished.

When you use the potty by yourself, how do you feel?

WASHING HANDS

My busy hands get dirty.

Soap and water make them clean!

I scrub my palms and fingers

and the spaces in between.

What else can you do to keep germs from spreading?

USING TISSUES

My icky, sticky boogies
aren't meant for hands or clothes.
Instead I'll get a tissue
to clean my runny nose.

Drippy noses are yucky and spread germs. I blow hard into a tissue and pretend I'm blowing out birthday candles with my nose!

Pretend you are an elephant blowing your nose. What does it sound like?

COVERING SNEEZES

I can feel it coming on...

one big, loud ACHOO!

But I will sneeze into my arm

and not send germs to you.

Germs can make people sick. I always cough or sneeze into my elbow, never into my hand or into the air.

What do you say to someone after they sneeze?

TAKING A BATH

At bath time every evening,

I watch the water flow.

I splish and splash in bubbles,

and I wash from head to toe.

What are your favorite bath toys?

GOING TO BED

If I'm grumpy or I yawn,
it's time to rest my head.
Even if I don't feel tired,
it's best to head to bed.

I feel better when I get good sleep. It's also healthy for my brain and body and helps me grow.

What makes bedtime special for you?

SAYING HELLO AND GOODBYE

To greet someone, I say, "Hello" or "How are you?" or "Hi!" Then when it's time for me to leave, I wave and say, "Goodbye."

Saying hello and goodbye are nice ways to start or end a conversation or visit. People around the world say hello and goodbye in different ways.

How else can you say hello or goodbye besides with words?

SAYING PLEASE

I never say, "Hey, give me that!"

I know that isn't right.

Instead I say, "May I?" and "Please?"

because I am polite.

What is something you asked for recently? How did you ask?

SAYING THANK YOU

Thank you for the brand-new toy

and for the pizza slice.

Thank you for inviting me,

and thanks for being nice.

What are other ways to show thanks besides using words?

SAYING SORRY

At times I might be mean or rude

or even disobey,

but saying "sorry" helps to make

bad feelings go away.

Everybody makes mistakes.
Sometimes it's hard to admit when
I've done something wrong.
But saying "sorry" makes
everyone feel better.

How does it feel when someone tells you they are sorry?

USING YOUR WORDS

**At times I stomp or whine or cry
'til people hold their ears.
I'm calmer when I use my words—
and easier to hear.**

Sometimes I get mad and scream when I don't get my way. But people listen to me more when I calmly tell them what I want or feel.

When you get upset, what makes you feel better?

USING YOUR INSIDE VOICE

When I'm tempted to be loud,

I have to make a choice:

make my happy noise outside,

or use my inside voice.

When I'm outdoors, my big voice can fly away into the clouds. I use my quiet voice indoors, since it won't disturb people.

In what kinds of places is it best to use your inside voice?

MAKING NEW FRIENDS

I'm very good at making friends.

This is what I say:

"What's your name? How old are you?"

and "Would you like to play?"

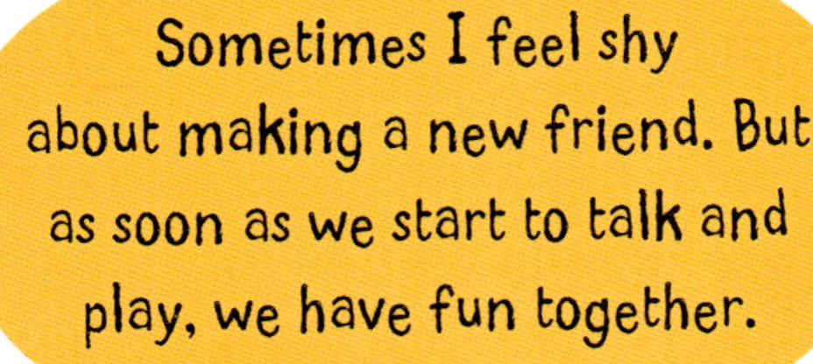

Do you have a best friend?

TELLING THE TRUTH

I always try to tell the truth,

and here's a reason why:

Everyone will trust me if

I do not tell a lie.

Even when I do something wrong, it's best to tell the truth. Telling a lie might feel easier, but telling the truth helps me grow and learn from my mistakes.

Has someone ever told you a lie? How did you feel?

LISTENING WHEN OTHERS TALK

I have a mouth so I can talk

to everyone all day.

I also have two ears to hear

what others have to say.

When your ears hear something you like, how does your face look?

NO NAME-CALLING

At times, I argue with my friends
when we are playing games.
But even if I'm really mad,
I never call them names.

How would you feel if someone called you a mean name?

FORGIVING OTHERS

If someone hurts my feelings,

or if they make me cry,

forgiving might be hard to do,

but I will always try.

Our feelings or bodies can get hurt by accident or on purpose. Forgiving means giving up the anger we feel after being hurt.

Have you ever hurt someone's feelings? Did they forgive you?

CROSSING THE STREET

I will hold a grown-up's hand

to go across the street.

I'll look both ways (not once, but twice)

before I move my feet.

If you are playing with a ball and it rolls into the street, what should you do?

DIALING 9-1-1

If someone's hurt or very sick,

I'll dial 9-1-1.

This call is for emergencies

and never just for fun!

Calling 9-1-1 is the way for an ambulance, fire truck, or police car to come and help us. A grown-up can teach me how to call properly.

What are some reasons you might call 9-1-1 for help?

NO TALKING TO STRANGERS

Strangers can be good or bad.

It's hard to tell, and so,

I'll never walk away alone

with someone I don't know!

I like meeting new people. But I only talk to grown-up strangers if I'm with a grown-up I trust.

If someone you don't know tries to call you over to them, what should you do?

NO TOUCHING HOT STOVES

Grown-ups always say to me,

"The stove is hot, hot, hot!"

When dinner comes, I'll finally see

what's in the pot, pot, pot!

How can you help cook or bake without going near the stove?

CLOSING CABINETS AND DRAWERS

Open, shut. Open, shut.

Every day and night.

After using drawers and doors,

I always close them tight.

When cabinets, doors, and drawers are left open, people can bump into them and get hurt. There are also some I should not open without asking first.

What cabinets and drawers have you been told not to open?

NO OBJECTS IN NOSE OR EARS

Only sounds go in my ears,

and up my nose, just air.

No beads or straws or dinosaurs

should ever go in there!

How many holes can you count on your head?

CLOSING THE DOOR BEHIND YOU

If I forget to shut the door

when I go out to play,

the bugs and heat come in the house

and pets might run away!

Closing the door keeps outside things out and inside things in. It helps everyone stay safe.

What would happen if you didn't have a door on your home?

PUTTING TOYS AWAY

Toys are all around the room.

I had such fun today!

Now I'll pick them up and sing

while I put them away.

What happens when you don't pick up your toys?

WIPING YOUR FEET

Before I go into the house,

I always wipe my feet.

That leaves the outside dirt behind

and keeps the inside neat.

STAYING NEAR YOUR FAMILY

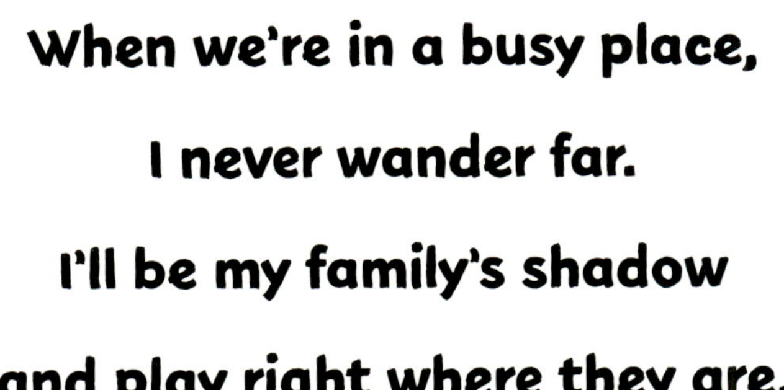

When we're in a busy place,
I never wander far.
I'll be my family's shadow
and play right where they are.

What should you do if you get lost in a busy place?

LEARNING YOUR HOME ADDRESS

I can learn my home address.

I'll sing it in a song!

I'll teach it to my teddy bear,

so he can sing along.

I can sing my address to the tune of one of my favorite songs. That will make it easy to remember if someone needs to help me get home if I'm lost.

Can you also learn your parent's phone number in a song?

AVOIDING POISONS

Some things look like candy or

a yummy kind of drink,

but nothing goes into my mouth

that's underneath the sink!

BEING SAFE AROUND DOGS

Some dogs bite and others jump.

They don't all want to play.

And so, before I pet a dog,

I ask if it's okay.

What do you like best about dogs?

NO KEEPING BAD SECRETS

A secret can be fun to keep,
unless it makes me scared.
So if I am uncomfortable,
that secret should be shared.

Good secrets, like a birthday surprise, will soon make people happy. Bad secrets make you feel hurt, unsafe, or unhappy, and should be told to a grown-up you trust.

Who would you go to if you needed to share a bad secret?

BEING SAFE NEAR WATER

It's fun to play in water,

but there's one important rule:

Always be with grown-ups

by the tub, the beach, or pool.

FOLLOWING RULES

There are rules at home and school.

Grown-ups have them too!

Rules reveal what's right and wrong,

so I'll know what to do.

What are some rules that you and your family follow?

DEALING WITH ANGRY FEELINGS

When I'm super-duper mad,

I slowly count to ten.

I breathe in deeply as I count

until I'm calm again.

Counting to ten gives me time to think instead of yelling or crying right away. Deep breaths make me feel calmer too.

When you're angry, what does it feel like in your body?

RESPECTING PERSONAL SPACE

Sometimes friends will want a hug

and other times they won't.

So I'll respect another's space

whenever they say, "Don't."

If I don't feel like getting a hug, I say so. Maybe later I'll change my mind. Everyone has their own feelings about hugs.

Who gives the best hugs?

TAKING TURNS

Taking turns is good to do.

I think you can agree.

There's lots of time for us to play

so you go first, then me.

When I really want to do something, it's very hard to wait my turn. But taking turns means everyone can share in the fun!

Has a friend ever let you go first? How did that feel?

BEING GENTLE WITH PETS

I love pets, like cats and dogs.

I never grab or smack.

I gently stroke and kindly pat.

That's why they love me back!

How do you play with your favorite pet?

SHOWING GRATITUDE

The rain has stopped. It's time to play.

I'm grateful for the sun.

And when I get to see my friends,

I'm thankful for the fun!

Having gratitude means to feel thankful for all the good things in my life. I am grateful for my home, food, and toys, and for the people who love me.

What are you grateful for?

HELPING OTHERS

I help my friends if they fall down.

At home, I help with chores.

When someone has a lot of bags,

I gladly open doors.

What are some ways you like to help others?

NO DRAWING ON WALLS

I made a pretty painting of

a flower, dog, and heart.

I drew on paper (not the wall)

to make my work of art!

Painting and drawing on furniture and walls can make a big mess. But my masterpieces look beautiful when hung on the wall or the fridge.

What kind of artwork do you like to create?

NO LITTERING

It makes me sad to see the trash

that people leave around.

So I won't be a litterbug and

toss things on the ground.

I throw wrappers and empty containers in the trash can or recycle bin. That keeps the Earth cleaner and happier!

What can you do if there is no trash can around outside?

SHARING WHAT'S YOURS

"Would you like to try my snack or come play with my toys?" Sharing can begin friendships with other girls and boys.

Did you share something today? Did someone share with you?

NO HITTING

Everybody fights sometimes,

but hurting isn't fair.

I know it's mean to hit or shove

or pull on someone's hair.

I don't like to be hurt, so I shouldn't hurt others either. If I'm angry, it's much better to use my words.

When you feel like hurting someone else, what could you do instead?

LEARNING FROM STORIES

My elders tell me stories of their lives from long ago. When I listen to their tales, it helps me learn and grow.

What interesting stories have older people told you?

CELEBRATING DIFFERENCES

I have friends who look like me

and others who do not.

But what's the thing that we all share?

We like each other lots!

GOODBYE POEM

I'm happy, healthy, safe, and kind
with what I do and say.
I'm growing big and strong and smart
through tiny steps each day!

What do you want to be when you grow up?

RACHELLE BURK is the author of fiction and nonfiction books for children, including *Sing, Hum, Strum, and Drum: My First Book of Music*, and *Stomp, Wiggle, Clap, and Tap: My First Book of Dance*. She lives in New Jersey and loves visiting schools around the country. Visit her at rachelleburk.com.

DENISE HOLMES is a champion hula-hooper and an award-winning freelance illustrator. Denise loves creating playful and colorful illustrations, especially for baby board books, bringing joy and wonder to little readers. In addition to drawing, Denise enjoys crafting, taking walks, reading, making pancakes, and writing in her diary. She lives in the heart of Chicago, IL, with her family.

Text by Rachelle Burk
Illustrations by Denise Holmes

The full color art was created using paper and pencil, Procreate, and Photoshop.

Published by Sourcebooks eXplore, an imprint of Sourcebooks Kids
1935 Brookdale RD, Naperville, IL 60563-2773
(630) 961-3900
sourcebooks.com

Cataloging-in-Publication Data is on file with the Library of Congress.

Source of Production: 1010 Printing Asia Limited, Kwun Tong, Hong Kong, China
Date of Production: December 2025
Run Number: 5058338

Printed and bound in China.
OGP 10 9 8 7 6 5 4 3 2 1

I am kind.

I am healthy.

I AM AWESOME!

I am safe.

I am kind.

I am safe.

I am healthy.

I AM AWESOME!

I am kind.

I am safe.

I AM AWESOME!

I am healthy.